THE LITTLE BOOK OF
CHEESE JOKES

THE LITTLE BOOK OF CHEESE JOKES

Copyright © Summersdale Publishers Ltd, 2015

With research by Owen Adams

Illustrations © Shutterstock

Summersdale Publishers Ltd
46 West Street
Chichester
West Sussex
PO19 1RP
UK

www.summersdale.com

Printed and bound in Malta

ISBN: 978-1-84953-859-6

Substantial discounts on bulk quantities of Summersdale books are available to corporations, professional associations and other organisations. For details contact Nicky Douglas by telephone: +44 (0) 1243 756902, fax: +44 (0) 1243 786300 or email: nicky@summersdale.com.

THE LITTLE BOOK OF CHEESE JOKES

Jake Harris

summersdale

WHICH IS THE MOST RELIGIOUS CHEESE?

SWISS, BECAUSE IT IS HOLY.

Which cheese is made backwards?

Edam.

What happened after an explosion at a French cheese factory?

All that was left was de Brie.

When cheese lovers play hide-and-seek, which nationality always wins?

....

The Dutch, because a Gouda man is hard to find.

What do you call cheese that is sad?

....

Blue cheese.

CHEESY FACT

In 1170, Henry II purchased 10,420 pounds of Cheddar, for a farthing a pound.

CHEESY READS

The Man in the Iron Mascarpone

....

The Havarti is a Provolonely Hunter

....

The Old Man and the Brie

....

Fromage to Catalonia

....

Jane Gruyère

....

Cheese Scone with the Wind

HOW DO YOU GET A MOUSE TO SMILE?

SAY 'CHEESE!'

What do you call cheese that isn't yours?

Nacho cheese!

Which cheese should you take to Wimbledon?

A tennis raclette.

CHEESY TUNES

'My Whey'

....

'Hit the Road, Monterey Jack'

....

'Paneerer, My God, to Thee'

....

'Babybel, I Love You'

....

'Red Red Rind'

....

'I Queso Girl and I Liked It'

CHEESY FACT

Casu Marzu is a cheese for only the bravest of dairy lovers: it's best eaten when its soft centre is full of live, wriggling maggots.

What is a cannibal's favourite cheese?

Limburger.

What did the blind man say after being handed a cheese grater?

'That's the most violent book I've ever read.'

**WHY DID THE
THREE KINGS ONLY
PACK TINY SLICES
OF BREAD FOR THEIR
SANDWICHES WHEN
THEY WENT TO
BETHLEHEM?**

....

**BECAUSE THEY WERE
GOING TO SEE THE
BABY CHEESES.**

Why did the dairy farmer go on a diet?

She wanted to Cheddar few pounds!

Which search engine is popular among mice?

Ask Cheese.

CHEESY MOVIES

A Room with a Fondue

....

Body Double Gloucester

....

There's Something About Dairy

....

The Full Nine Yargs

....

A Beautiful Rind

....

The Roquefort Horror Picture Show

CHEESY FACT

The largest slice of cheese ever churned was unveiled in 2007 by a New York cheese shop and a Danish cheesemaker. It weighed 1,323 pounds and measured 6 feet wide.

What's the most dangerous part of the Atlantic Ocean for boats carrying dairy products?

The Bermuda Cheese Triangle.

What is Tom Hanks' favourite soft cheese?

Philadelphia.

CHEESY TUNES

'Hello – Is It Brie You're Looking For?'

....

'I Stilton Haven't Found What I'm
Looking For'

....

'It's in His Quiche'

....

'Ricotta Get Out of This Place'

....

'Sgt Pepper's Lonely Havarti's
Club Band'

....

'I'm a Brieliever'

WHOM DID THE CHEESY BIBLE START WITH?

....

EDAM AND EVE.

What kind of cheese do horror-movie fans enjoy?

Gore-gonzola.

Which hotel do mice stay in?

The Stilton.

What did the cheese salesman say?

That cheese may be Gouda, but this one is feta!

Which kind of cheese has been known to fly?

Curds of prey!

CHEESY FACT

If you order a dish called 'Halve Hahn', or 'half a rooster', in Cologne, Germany, you won't get a poultry feast but half a bread roll with a slice of cheese on the top.

CHEESY READS

Rosemary's Babybel

....

The Third Manchego

....

The Secret Dairy of Adrian Mole,
Aged 13¾

....

Rarebit, Run

....

Fifty Shades of Brie

....

The Curious Incident of the Yarg
in the Night-Time

WHAT IS THE NAME OF THE COUNTRY NEAR IRAQ THAT IS MADE ENTIRELY OF CHEESE?

....

CURD-ISTAN.

What cheese surrounds a medieval castle?

Moatzarella.

What dance do cheesemakers do every Halloween?

The Munster mash!

CHEESY TUNES

'I Curd It Through the Grapevine'

....

'You Spin Me Rind (Like a Record)'

....

'In-A-Gouda-Da-Vida'

....

'Gouda Night Irene'

....

'The Gratest Love of All'

....

'Personal Cheeses'

CHEESY FACT

The British eat around 700,000 tonnes of cheese every year! But the French, Italians and Germans eat twice as much: they have 65 g per day, while the Brits eat only 30 g per day.

Which cheese should you use to hide a horse?

Mascarpone.

Which Welsh cheese must you always eat with caution?

Caerphilly.

WHY DID THE ONE-LEGGED CLOWN LEAVE THE CHEESE CIRCUS?

BECAUSE HE COULDN'T GET HIS STILTON.

How does a cycling cheesemonger carry her wares around?

Using paneers.

What does a lady in a mall do with a cheesy credit card?

Go on a shopping Brie.

CHEESY MOVIES

Three Men and a Babybel

....

The Hunt for Red Leicester

....

Cheeses of Nazareth

....

Swiss Cheese Family Robinson

....

As Gouda As It Gets

....

Les Amants du Pont Neufchatel

CHEESY FACT

A study carried out by the British Cheese Board revealed no evidence for the popular myth that cheese gives you nightmares. In fact, most of the 200 participants reported a good night's sleep with pleasant dreams.

Why did the cheese doctor like looking at the Stilton?

Because it had such beautiful veins.

What is a lion's favourite cheese?

Roar-quefort.

CHEESY SPORTS

A-feta-letics

The 110 m Curdles

Primula One

Cracker Barrel Racing

Leerdammer Throw

Racletteball

White Water Biscuit Rafting

WHAT DO YOU CALL A CHEESE FROM THE FAR EAST?

....

PARM-ASIAN.

What did the piece of Cheddar say to the ghost?

I'm Lac-ghost intolerant.

Which genre of music appeals to most cheeses?

R'n'Brie.

What did the doctor say to the poorly cheese?

I'm sure you'll feel feta soon.

Which cheese do beavers like?

Edam.

CHEESY FACT

During the Roman Empire, large houses had a separate kitchen for manufacturing cheese, called a *careale*.

CHEESY MOVIES

Cheese Just Not That Into You

....

Fried Gruyère Tomatoes

....

Where Eagles Dairy

....

Brie with Mussolini

....

The Mozzarellaphant Man

....

Swiss of the Spider Woman

WHY DID THE CHEESE LOOK SANE?

....

BECAUSE THE REST OF THE PLATE WAS CRACKERS.

Which is the richest cheese in the world?

Paris Stilton.

What's the most popular American cheese sitcom?

Curd Your Enthusiasm.

CHEESY TUNES

'I Don't Like Montereys'

'I'll Brie There for You'

'Like a Puppet on a Cheesestring'

'Under the Cheeseboard Walk'

'Girls Just Wanna Have Fontina'

'Grate Balls of Fire'

CHEESY FACT

A connoisseur of cheese is known as a turophile.

WHAT DO CHEESE PHOTOGRAPHERS SAY WHEN TAKING A PICTURE?

....

'SAY HUMANS!'

What is a basketball player's favourite kind of cheese?

Swish cheese!

What do you say to a bear that is walking really slow and lagging behind?

Camembert!

What did the street cheese say after he got attacked by several blades?

I've felt grater.

What did the cheese say when it looked in the mirror?

Halloumi!

CHEESY MOVIES

The Whey Whey Back

Never Been Quiched

The Curd Man

Who Dairies Wins

Edambusters

The Gouda, the Bad and the Ugly

WHAT WAS THE NAME OF A FAMOUS CHEESE-LOVING FREEDOM FIGHTER?

CHÈVRE GUEVARA.

What do you call a grilled cheese sandwich that's all up in your face?

Too close for comfort food.

What's a cheese's favourite pantomime?

Mozzarella.

CHEESY TUNES

'Blue Cheese Suede Shoes'

....

'Roquefort the Law (and the Law Won)'

....

'Let It Brie'

....

'Johnny B. Gouda'

....

'A Yarg Day's Night'

....

'Feta the Devil You Know'

WHICH CHEESE IS ALWAYS DRUNK?

·····

MORBIER.

The early bird may get the worm, but the second mouse gets the cheese.

If I like you, I'll make you a cheese sandwich. If I love you, I'll grill it.

What was the punishment for Gouda Fawkes' crimes?

They put him on the raclette.

What's the best way to count cheese?

Using Emmental arithmetic.

CHEESY FACT

The official world record for the largest macaroni cheese ever made goes to a dish weighing 1,119.91 kg (2,469 lbs) that was served in Fulton Square, New Orleans on 23 September 2010.

CHEESY READS

Grate Expectations

The Cheese-and-Grapes of Wrath

Robinson Queso

The Rind of the Baskervilles

East of Edam

Quiche the Girls

KNOCK KNOCK.

WHO'S THERE?

CHEESE!

CHEESE WHO?

**CHEESE A JOLLY
GOOD FELLOW.**

What do sinful cheeses fear most of all?

Edamnation.

When blue cheeses come first in a sporting event, what do they win?

A mould medal.

CHEESY TUNES

'Sweet dreams are made of cheese,

Who am I to diss a Brie?

I Cheddar the world and the
feta cheese,

Everybody's looking for Stilton.'

CHEESY FACT

Lactococcus lactis, the bacterium used to make Cheddar and other hard cheeses, was honoured in 2010 as the official microbe of Wisconsin, America's no.1 cheese-producing state.

Which cheese will you always find physically closest to you?

Panear.

Why couldn't the police stop the Great Cheese Robbery from happening?

Because it was a feta compli.

A ROQUEFORT, A STILTON AND A CAMBOZOLA FORMED A BAND. WHAT TYPE OF MUSIC DID THEY PLAY?

....

THE BLUES!

Why did the male stripper feel so uncomfortable at the cheese-themed hen night?

Because the bride-to-be would Leerdammer.

What did the philosopher say to Elvis?

What's your Roquefort?

CHEESY MOVIES

Fromage Here to Eternity

....

The Goudafather

....

Käse-blanca

....

Halloumi, Myself and Irene

....

The Camembert Run

....

Brie Encounter

CHEESY FACT

The stinkiest cheese in the world is widely agreed to be Vieux-Boulogne, an unpasteurised cow's-milk cheese from France.

When is it easiest to see cheese?

When it goes pasteurised.

Which kind of cheese lives in a small house?

Cottage cheese.

CHEESY READS

The Cheese Merchant of Venice

....

A Brie History of Time

....

The Lord of the Rinds

....

Everything is Hallouminated

....

The Comté of Monte Cristo

....

Brighton Roquefort

**DID YOU HEAR ABOUT
THE CHEESEMAKER
WHO PAINTED HIS
WIFE TWICE? HE
DOUBLE GLOUCESTER!**

When should you keep an eye on your cheese?

When you think it might be up to no Gouda.

What's a zombie's favourite cheese?

Monsterella!

Why can't you sleep, son?

Because there's a Munster under my bed.

I used to work as a cheesemonger, but I Camembert it any longer.

CHEESY FACT

The world's only moose-milk cheese is produced in Bjursholm, Sweden. It's pricey, though – just under $1,000 per kilo!

CHEESY MOVIES

Brie Men and a Little Lady

....

Fromage to the Centre of the Earth

....

Feta Off Dead

....

Where the Buffalo Mozzarella Roam

....

Gruyère Window

....

À La Recherche du Temps Fondue

WHAT DID THE OUT-OF-DATE CHEDDAR SAY TO HIS FRIENDS?

....

DON'T WORRY, I'M JUST FEELING A BIT CHEESED OFF.

What do you call a cheese that is an alcoholic?

Livarot.

What did John McEnroe say when the umpire dropped his cheese sandwich?

You cannot Brie serious!

CHEESY READS

Cheddar Gabler

....

The Scarlet Feta

....

Peter Paneer

....

The Men Who Stare at Goat's Cheese

....

For Whom the Bel Paese Tolls

....

The Voyage of the Dawn Cheddar

CHEESY FACT

Believe it or not, mice don't really like cheese, and they actively avoid smelly cheeses.

Why did the cheese become pregnant?

She was prophylactose intolerant.

Which detective show solves cheese crimes?

The Roquefort Files.

WHY WAS THE CHEESE SENT HOME FROM THE TRENCHES?

HIS NEUFS WERE COMPLETELY CHATELLED.

When are a cheese's formative years?

Fromage 3–7.

What's the most sought-after cheesy part of the British Isles?

The Welsh rare bit.

CHEESY MOVIES

The Curd Locker

....

The Grate Escape

....

Munsters, Inc.

....

Gouda Will Hunting

....

The Five-Gruyère Engagement

....

The Bangkok Stilton

WHAT DO YOU GET WHEN YOU CROSS A SMURF AND A COW?

....

BLUE CHEESE!

What precaution should men take in case they need to look smart at work?

Always Havarti.

What did the cheese say when it disguised itself as a frog?

'Rennet, rennet.'

CHEESY READS

The Beautiful and Edammed

The Curious Queso of Benjamin Button

The Käse-Book of Sherlock Holmes

Far From the Madding Curd

Ulys-cheese

Bridget Jones's Dairy

WHY DO AGEING STILTONS WEAR THICK STOCKINGS?

TO HIDE THEIR VARICOSE VEINS.

Where is Gene Pitney?

Provolone 24 hours from Tulsa.

Why did the Spanish cheese leave the party?

He was feeling a bit queso.

Where do Austrians keep their icebergs?

....

In a Bergkäse.

What type of car does a cheese prefer?

....

A Chevrèlet.

DO CHEESES BELIEVE IN FREE WILL?

....

NO, THEY'RE TOO FETALISTIC.

CHEESY MOVIES

The Guns of Mascarpone

·····································

From Here to Maturity

·····································

*Harry Ricotta and the Prisoner
of Parmesan*

·····································

Memoirs of a Gouda

·····································

Fromage Of Innocence

·····································

Cheese the One

WHAT DID GUSTAVE FLAUBERT SAY TO HIS FRIEND ÉMILE WHEN THEY WERE WALKING ALONG A CHEESY BEND IN THE ROAD TOGETHER?

'CAREFUL. WE'RE ON A STEEP CAMBOZOLA.'

CHEESY FACT

Queen Victoria was given a wheel of Cheddar that weighed half a tonne as a wedding gift.

What does a cheese become when it falls out with its friends?

Persona non gratin.

Why was the Belgian waiter fired after he served the cheese course?

He was being a bit too Chimay with the guests.

WHO'S THE CHEESIEST CHARACTER IN THE *STAR WARS* MOVIES?

·····································

BOBA FETA.

JOKES
for all the
FAMILY

Harry Hilton

JOKES FOR ALL THE FAMILY

Harry Hilton

£7.99
Paperback
ISBN: 978-1-84953-273-0

Did you hear about the schoolboy who put clean socks on every day?

By Friday he couldn't get his shoes on.

Prepare to have your ribs tickled, your funny bone waggled and your leg pulled with this bumper compendium of jokes for all the family. With everything from ludicrous lions to preposterous pirates, there are laughs aplenty for everyone!

If you're interested in finding out more about our books, find us on Facebook at **Summersdale Publishers** and follow us on Twitter at **@Summersdale**.

www.summersdale.com